IN OLD PHOTOGR ~~BRITAI~~

C000088673

ASHFORD

THEN & NOW

STEVE R. SALTER

Steve Salter 2004

SUTTON PUBLISHING

Sutton Publishing Limited
Phoenix Mill · Thrupp · Stroud
Gloucestershire · GL5 2BU

First published 2004

Title page photograph: Aerial view, north-west sector, 1977. This superb view shows the continuing redevelopment into the late 1970s. A new Sainsbury's supermarket can be seen under construction (centre) and, to the left, the well-known Ashdown Court development is in its foundation stage. The street 'cornering' the bottom left of the picture is Albert Road. (*FotoFlite*)

British Library Cataloguing in Publication Data
A catalogue record for this book is available from the British Library.

ISBN 0-7509-3924-9

Typeset in 10.5/13.5 Photina.
Typesetting and origination by
Sutton Publishing Limited.
Printed and bound in England by
J.H. Haynes & Co. Ltd, Sparkford.

Dedicated to Mum, Dad and James

In memory of Tom Hall, former Curator of Ashford Museum:
One of life's original true gentlemen

St George's Square, 1950. A peaceful postwar view of St George's Square, showing the tank (centre) and the Old Prince of Wales public house on the right. The trees shading the tank are long gone, and in recent years a protective cover has been built to preserve the landmark from the elements. Nowadays the square is traffic-free. (*Ashford Borough Council*)

CONTENTS

Tufton Street, 1970. Five years before the opening of the Tufton Shopping Centre, Tufton Street was still a through road linking with many streets including Hempsted Street and Apsley Street. This rare view shows the Coach and Horses public house in the distance, Trice's the florist and greengrocer on the left and Nicholas Kingsman the Kentish Bakers (who also ran a shop in New Rents) on the right. Alongside the post office (centre) is the Elwick Club, and opposite were the almshouses (which later moved to Vicarage Lane). After the construction of the shopping centre, everything past the post office was demolished. The Elwick Club later relocated to new purpose-built premises in Church Road. *(Ashford Borough Council)*

INTRODUCTION

The Ashford we all know and recognise today is a far cry from the historic market and railway town it once was. The railway works are now largely derelict pending redevelopment and the cattle market having moved out of town in recent years are clear indications that Ashford past is fast becoming Ashford future. Although still extremely popular with Ashfordians and visitors from all over the south-east and further afield, much of Ashford's everyday trade has been spread far and wide, and not only local firms but also large and well-known national and international businesses now occupy many of Ashford's surrounding greenfield sites. For example many will remember companies such as Tesco, whose first Ashford

Tufton Centre, Central Square, 1979. Tesco Home and Wear store, which opened in 1975, was one of the original tenants of the Tufton Centre. Sadly for many shoppers, the store closed its doors in August 1987, and the premises became a new store for the Littlewoods chain. (*Ashford Borough Council*)

supermarket opened in the town in 1975, then in the newly opened Tufton Shopping Centre. They opened their first new-build out-of-town store in 1988 in Willesborough, adjacent to the M20 motorway, a year after closing their town centre store. Sainsbury's had many different locations in the town, their first in 1934 in the High Street, but eventually moved out of town, concentrating on their superstore which opened in 1992. Other trades including DIY stores, electrical stores and restaurants have found it more feasible to move away from the heart of the town, causing at the time, and even today, mixed opinions from many local residents.

However, in times past the streets, trades and everyday scenes in the town also changed from one era to another, sometimes in a matter of months. Many familiar sites in the town may be totally transformed – and even disappear completely – compared to how they once looked, mainly thanks to redevelopment. The effect is that whole areas can fade from our memories, and this has happened as an ongoing process in Ashford over the last thirty years. Ashfordians have certainly had to come to terms with the expression 'Out with the old and in with the new!'

There are some exciting projects happening to Ashford over the next few years and beyond, in many respects to bring the town further and further up to date, but planners are adamant that Ashford's remaining historical aspects will not be obliterated any more. It's a terrible shame that this anti-demolition stance wasn't taken twenty or so years ago. Again as readers who have taken an interest in my previous work, *Changing Ashford*, will notice, many of the comparative photographs are specifically dated, and every possible effort has been made to take present-day equivalent pictures of sites in the same position as in the past. Unfortunately this has been difficult on occasions, particularly when standing in the centre of a main road, but nevertheless it has been a rewarding and worthwhile challenge. Those who have a passion for Ashford's past will appreciate that, if it wasn't for the invention of the camera, and the dedication of many photographers who took these splendid pictures, we would find it very hard to picture our memories of Ashford, and remember days gone by.

Remember these?

Steve R. Salter
November 2004

Aerial view, 1970. A cloudy day taken from the church tower of St Mary's, showing North Street before the Ringway divided it, creating a no through road from its junction with Somerset Road. Beyond the trees is the old Ashford bypass, which opened in 1957, and twenty-five years later became part of the M20 motorway. Kennington can also be seen in the distance, and was still very under-developed compared to today. Although not illustrated, the site on which Charter House now stands was yet to be developed in 1970. Work started the following year. The modern building (bottom left) was purpose-built for J. Sainsbury in 1966 as their first Ashford self-service supermarket. Up till then they ran a smaller counter service store at 18 High Street (now part of NatWest bank), which opened in 1934. The site of their 1966 store on the corner of High Street and North Street was previously occupied for many years by the Saracen's Head Hotel. *(Jim Ashby)*

1

Charting the Changes

New Rents, 20 August 1975. Many Ashfordians will remember Lewis & Hyland's for its old-fashioned values. Its many departments including haberdashery, menswear, ladieswear and childrenswear made it a popular shop to many generations past. Even when its premises in New Rents were demolished in the late 1970s, they continued their established trade in new premises in the Tufton Shopping Centre (now County Square) until the early 1980s when they ceased trading. This picture was taken shortly before its demolition for phase two of the redevelopment of Hempsted Street. (Jim Ashby)

New Rents, July 2004. Today New Rents is hardly recognisable from the photograph on the left. The buildings here were erected as part of phase two of the Tufton Shopping Centre, by local construction firm C.I. Epps. Whereas previously Lewis & Hyland dominated this part of New Rents, it now houses a Carphone Warehouse, Scope charity shop and Argos, among others. (Steve Salter)

Opposite, top: New Rents, 29 February 1976. Gerald Brown, fruiterer and greengrocer, was a familiar name in the 1970s for fresh fruit and veg. Based at the top of New Rents the premises were previously those of A.E. Gibbs the baker and were directly opposite H.J. Davis the pork butcher. Gerald Brown gave way to Creative Interiors in the 1980s. (Jim Ashby)

Opposite, bottom: New Rents, July 2004. After having played host to a number of trades after Creative Interiors, including GZ Computers and Bar España, nos 18–20 recently opened as UnDecided Bar/Café and eating outlet, creating something of a pleasant change, offering music and entertainment to people of all ages. (Steve Salter)

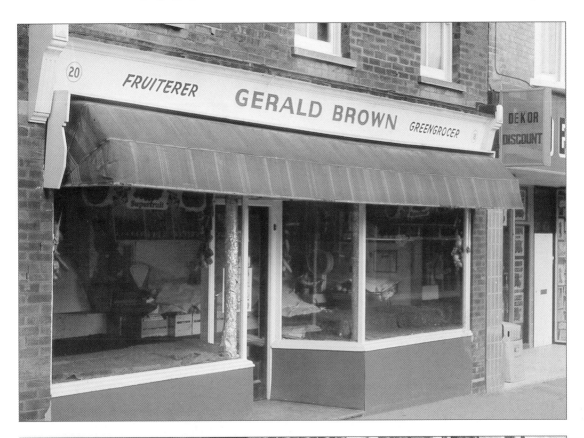

New Rents, 29 February 1976. This is another forgotten business, A.C. & M.F.E. Maple, tobacconist, at 4 New Rents. Previously the shop had been owned by A.R. Doughty and was opposite Lewis & Hyland's department store at 7 New Rents. The familiar shopfront disappeared and has changed considerably; in recent years the premises have been a bank. *(Jim Ashby)*

New Rents, July 2004. The Romanian Hospice Appeal shop now occupies no. 4. As you can see from the appearance there is no comparison to that of Maple's, and today the shop looks bigger. This is one of many charity shops in this part of Ashford. *(Steve Salter)*

Opposite, top: New Rents junction with Hempsted Street, 31 July 1975. Adjacent to Lewis & Hyland's store stood Nicholas Kingsman the bakers, on the opposite corner to Frank Palmer the outfitters at the top of Hempsted Street. Kingsman's also at one time had premises in Bank Street, and when they had to vacate this building for its demolition, took premises in the Tufton Shopping Centre. Interestingly Nicholas Kingsman does exist, and I believe he was a baby when the business was named. *(Jim Ashby)*

Opposite, bottom: New Rents, July 2004. It's difficult to pinpoint exactly where Kingsmans stood, but it was roughly where Pet Essentials (formerly Dixons) now stands. Today there is nothing left of the Hempsted Street end of New Rents. *(Steve Salter)*

New Street, 14 February 1982. Many people will fondly remember E. Collins' Tank Milk Bar at 3–5 New Street, to many an important part of their teenage years, as it was a meeting point not just for youngsters but for businessmen and people of all ages. In this photograph the Tanduri Indian curry house occupies the premises. Next door Knowles furniture department occupies no. 7, which for many years previously had been Daniels (Kent) Ltd, estate agents, auctioneers and valuers. Ashford Cycle Centre was previously Jack Scott's second-hand bargain shop and Gouldens wool shop. On the corner of Gilbert Road stood A. Sellers & Son, the well-known local butcher, which up to its closure was one of the last local butcher's shops to have sawdust on the floor and where the staff wore the traditional striped aprons. *(Jim Ashby)*

New Street, July 2004. A post-pedestrianised view of New Street showing nos 3–5 now occupied by Ashford Bengal Cuisine. Knowles have given way more recently to the late-night Source bar, whereas Wells Clinic, Independent Life and Seekers Lettings occupy 9, 11 and 13 New Street. *(Steve Salter)*

Castle Street, 2 November 1980. A late afternoon view of Castle Street looking towards the Tank and the Old Prince of Wales public house. No. 3, seen here as Ashford Models, was once the premises of Jack Guy, the popular Ashford pork butcher. Knowles at nos 5–7 was a well-known name in Ashford for many generations but disappeared in the early 1980s. They also had premises in New Street and at 106 High Street, which were demolished in the late 1970s to make way for the Provincial Building Society (now Toni & Guy hairdressers). F.J. Dean, turf accountants, had previously been in Park Street, but their premises made way for a widening scheme in 1974. Next door Merry's newsagent and tobacconist continued its trade until the early 1990s. *(Jim Ashby)*

Castle Street, July 2004. Not one of those businesses remains twenty-four years later. Topps Jewellery now occupies no. 3, while F.J. Dean has been succeeded by Coral and has moved into larger premises where Knowles once were. Their old premises are now occupied by adult shop Pillow Talk, and Merry's at no. 11 has now become Elite Menswear, dealing in quality designer menswear. They also have a shop in Canterbury. *(Steve Salter)*

North Street, 29 January 1984. Denne's (or T. Denne & Sons as they are also known) is one of the best-known corn and seed merchants in Kent and particularly in the town for their retail store, which once occupied 6–10 North Street. They succeeded Hart & Tapnall of the same trade. The building was refurbished in the early 1980s, which saw the closure of the separate florist's shop, and its letting to become DGH Computer software. Denne's closed their retail business in the mid-1980s and the premises became Supersaver Discount Stores and Shoe Rack. Latterly Supersaver became Top Notch, and in 1997 a devastating fire all but destroyed the building originally built in 1883. (*Jim Ashby*)

North Street, July 2004. After standing derelict and open to the elements for seven years, the burned-out shell of nos 6–10 has been purchased by two Chinese businessmen. They have sympathetically rebuilt the property, which is soon to become a Chinese buffet restaurant. The brothers Alan and Roland Yeung also have reputable businesses in Chatham and Faversham. (*Steve Salter*)

North Street, 14 February 1982. Another of Ashford's long-lost trades is Ashley Russell Ltd, milliners and costumiers at 2 North Street. The building, which is an extension to 54 High Street, is one of great splendour when viewed from its interior. On the first floor there is a round balustrade opening looking down on the ground floor, and there are a series of small rooms on the first and second, one of which was a café many years ago, and still retains its original dumb waiter, round-backed cupboards and Wright's cast-iron fireplace. Ashley Russell's was well known for its quality and tradition in ladies' clothing. It closed in 1984. *(Jim Ashby)*

North Street, July 2004. Until recently and since Ashley Russell closed, the first and second floors were never fully utilised, owing to fire regulations. The Merchant Chandler changed all that and once again the upper floors are in use. After extensive refurbishment, they opened their shop in late 2003 selling bric-a-brac, furniture, rugs and all sorts of quality merchandise for the home. *(Steve Salter)*

Tufton Street, 15 June 1975. The Swan public house in Tufton Street was originally a coaching inn. At one time it was a familiar haunt in the town centre for policemen, as it was just opposite their Ashford headquarters. Years ago the inn was owned by Style & Winch and latterly Courage, but after Courage sold off their many pubs all over Kent, it was first bought by Acorn Inns of Tunbridge Wells and then taken over by the Balham firm Pubs 'n' Bars. *(Jim Ashby)*

Tufton Street, July 2004. Still looking much the same, the Swan is now young person-orientated. Managed by Lyn Sumner, with the assistance of her faithful son Dean, the Swan is always extremely busy, and has for many years welcomed a regular clientele. *(Steve Salter)*

Bank Street, 14 February 1982. The lower section of Bank Street has in recent years been an area for restaurants and wine bars. Here the Trattoria Romana, which at one time was W. & B. Hobbs, auctioneers, valuers and estate agents, is seen next door to Corkers wine bar. Corkers had been absent from the town after its closure several years ago until recently, when the name was temporarily revived. The Shelter shop at 28 Bank Street is adjacent to the Centrepiece and the Bank Street Methodist Church. (*Jim Ashby*)

Bank Street, July 2004. The new Corkers sadly didn't prove fruitful, but in its place Threezero opened, offering a bar, kitchen and DJ, in its state-of-the-art refurbished premises. The Trattoria Romana is also still a popular eating venue twenty-two years on. (*Steve Salter*)

Bank Street, 29 April 1979. This is a memorable view of Upper Bank Street, in the days when buses used to stop outside the shops. The wool shop on the left, owned by Mrs Evernden, traded until the late 1980s after having been there for many years and supplying decades of knitters. The Woolwich Building Society is seen here trading in the former Strange's premises. They were drapers and milliners, and also occupied no. 6 next door, latterly Butler & Hatch Waterman, estate agents. Leavers' tobacconist and confectioner also had premises in New Street and Middle Row. All were owned by popular businessman Mr C.J. Leaver. *(Jim Ashby)*

Bank Street, July 2004. The Woolwich later extended their bank into no. 6 after County Group estate agents (successor to Butler & Hatch Waterman) vacated the premises. Barnardo's book store was at no. 10a for only a short time, and the shop with the blind, Barry's Kitchen, is popular with business people and shoppers at lunchtime, serving quality take-away food, including pastries and savouries at all times. *(Steve Salter)*

Bank Street junction with Godinton Road, 28 September 1975. Wright Brothers, sports outfitters, were a familiar name in Ashford for many years. Their premises at 38 Bank Street stood on this corner. They later had premises at 55 High Street, which had previously been Rabson's Toy Shop. Mr Keston-Hole managed Wright Brothers for many years. No. 38 was also the Oxfam shop at one time. *(Jim Ashby)*

Bank Street junction with Godinton Road, July 2004. After Montag Leisure acquired the building from Oxfam, no. 38 was in a bad state of repair. The building was subsequently extensively refurbished and now houses Montag's Gaming Centre. *(Steve Salter)*

Bank Street, 21 April 1985. A deserted view of Bank Street, probably taken on a Sunday. The Alliance Building Society at 19 Bank Street was once the Ashford Trustee Savings Bank. Next door Britannia Building Society was once Foster, Finn-Kelcey, chartered accountants, and next door where William Hill's betting shop still stands today, Freeman Hardy & Willis once ran their boot and shoe retailers before moving to the former premises of Vye and Sons, grocers, at 58 High Street. *(Jim Ashby)*

Bank Street, July 2004. Nothing much has changed in eighteen years apart from the obvious, for example the introduction of railings and traffic lights. A few years ago Ashford Borough Council were looking at plans to divert the buses to Park Street and totally pedestrianise the lower part of Bank Street. *(Steve Salter)*

Bank Street, 12 September 1976. Almost forgotten, another of Ashford's past clothing retailers, Victor's Fashions at 5 Bank Street were also known as costumiers and milliners. They were similar in trade to Ashley Russell's and James & Kither, but according to this 1976 photograph they were up for sale. No. 5 later became the home of the Halifax Building Society. *(Jim Ashby)*

Bank Street, July 2004. When the Halifax moved to new premises at the former Castle Inn at 1 Castle Street in 1997, 5 Bank Street became an extension to the offices of Kingsford's solicitors (formerly Kingsford, Flower & Pain). *(Steve Salter)*

Bank Street junction with Tufton Street, 12 September 1976. Hard to remember now, but this is how Bank Street looked in 1976. From left to right: Jeans and Things at no. 16, Carousel toys at no. 14, Gizzi café at no. 12 and C. Kingston Ltd, butcher, at no. 10. None of these businesses is still trading today. (*Jim Ashby*)

Bank Street junction with Tufton Street, July 2004. The top of Bank Street is now pedestrianised, and it is difficult to see some of the changes. Entry to the pedestrianised area is now restricted during office hours to permit holders and disabled shoppers. (*Steve Salter*)

Upper High Street, 29 April 1984. This cheerful spring scene shows the well-kept flowerbeds in the pedestrianised area of the Upper High Street. The drum-shaped advertising boards were familiar in Ashford during the 1970s and '80s. *(Jim Ashby)*

Upper High Street, July 2004. Recently made into a performance area, new trees and planting have been installed. This has brought the town centre up to date and organisations and traders regularly use the performance area. Much of this is managed by town centre manager Chris West. *(Steve Salter)*

Upper High Street, 15 June 1975. The George
Hotel at 68 High Street was and still is a central
meeting place in Ashford. There is said to be a
right of way through the doors into Park Street.
Marks & Spencer at 64–6 High Street is seen here
before moving up to the Tufton Centre in 1977.
During the war in 1943 members of the
American army were often seen in the Donut Club
(above Marks & Spencer) when off duty. (Jim Ashby)

Upper High Street, July 2004. The George Hotel
as it is today. It was one of three public houses in
the town which were once run by Mark and Gerry
Allibone, the others two being the Swan and the
County Hotel. The former Marks & Spencer
store was later remodelled and split, and now
houses Barclays Bank and Iceland frozen foods.
(Steve Salter)

Opposite, top: Upper High Street, 31 August 1980. Timothy Whites was another familiar name in
Ashford. Here they are occupying 70–2 High Street. The premises were previously occupied by Boots the
Chemist, which then moved to 60–2 High Street and in 1979 opened in the old J. Sainsbury branch at
56 High Street. When Timothy Whites later amalgamated with Boots, nos 70–2 became Boots Cookshop
and was demolished in 1986, to build a new W.H. Smith's. Next door the George Hotel is said to be one
of the oldest inns in Ashford. (Jim Ashby)

Opposite, bottom: Upper High Street. July 2004. W.H. Smith opened in 1987 in its brand new building,
replacing the former 70–2 High Street. Again the street has since been part-pedestrianised. (Steve Salter)

High Street (middle), 28 September 1975. Timothy Whites' other store was at 60–2 High Street, which also at one time had been Boots the Chemist. Inside, the shop had a grand wooden staircase, which was removed when these premises were split, creating a home for Quality Seconds, family wear, and Abbey National building society. Next door, Freeman, Hardy & Willis at no. 58 took over the former premises of Vye & Son Ltd, grocers. *(Jim Ashby)*

High Street (middle), July 2004. The attractive premises of 58, 60 and 62 High Street as they stand today. *(Steve Salter)*

Middle Row, 21 June 1975. Many Ashfordians will fondly remember C.W. Dixon & Co., the ironmonger and cutler at 7 Middle Row, who notched up over 75 years' trade in the town. Dixons were renowned for quality and used to hang their wares from their shopfront. They advertised that they sold 'tools for all trades', 'domestic hardware' and 'garden requisites'. Next door Bodsham's Farm Shop traded in the former Waghorne Butchers at 4 Middle Row. *(Jim Ashby)*

Middle Row, July 2004. After Dixons closed in the late 1970s no. 7 became a ladies' clothes shop and an off-licence, but was later knocked through as part of the Man of Kent public house. During the summer months the management provide outside seating for their customers to enjoy. *(Steve Salter)*

Middle Row, 21 June 1975. The original entrance to the Man of Kent public house, before it was extended and altered, creating a new entrance where Dixons' shop had been. *(Jim Ashby)*

Middle Row, July 2004. Nowadays the Man of Kent can slash their prices, advertising 'Everything under £2, Guaranteed, All Day Every Day!' Perhaps they should go back to 1975 prices? *(Steve Salter)*

Churchyard Passage, 25 March 1974. A peaceful scene of Churchyard Passage, showing the tower of the Church of St Mary the Virgin. At the time Rabsons toyshop was on the left and Thresher's off-licence on the right. *(Jim Ashby)*

Churchyard Passage, July 2004. Much the same view as thirty years ago, although mature trees are now visible. *(Steve Salter)*

Castle Street, 15 June 1975. The Castle Hotel, latterly the Castle, was once another of the town's coaching inns. At one time it boasted six bars. In more recent years it was known as a bikers' pub and was a popular venue for live bands. It sadly fell into disrepair and Shepherd Neame closed the Castle in 1996. The last landlord and landlady were Stuart Barton and Dee Martin. The Castle also changed its livery on numerous occasions over the years. *(Jim Ashby)*

Castle Street, July 2004. In 1997 the Castle was transformed into new premises for the Halifax. Extensive work was undertaken to underpin the crumbling building, which was in a worse state than estimated, and 1 Castle Street was given a new lease of life. *(Steve Salter)*

Upper High Street, 24 January 1988. A quiet day in the Upper High Street showing some of the businesses there at the time. Nos 96–8, previously H. Horton and Son, boot and shoe retailers, were taken over by K Shoes in 1966 and remained there till 1992. W.H. Smith Travel at 100 High Street had previously been Marcus Army & Navy Stores (Gravesend Ltd). Dewhurst the Butcher at 102 High Street had previously been Matthews Butchers, the Carpet Centre and Co-operative Chemist. Currys electrical stores at no. 104 had previously been James & Kither, drapers and milliners, and National & Provincial at 106 High Street was for many years Knowles and Co., house furnishers. *(Jim Ashby)*

Upper High Street, July 2004. A general view of today's businesses which include Toni & Guy, hairdressers, Zoom the Loom, home furnishings, Snappy Snaps, photo and digital specialists and O₂, mobile telephone store. *(Steve Salter)*

Upper High Street, 31 August 1980. The K Shoe Shop at 96–8 High Street now looks very dated. The shop was refurbished in 1986. *(Jim Ashby)*

Upper High Street, July 2004. The smart shop frontage of 96–8 High Street is now occupied by an O₂ mobile telephone outlet. *(Steve Salter)*

Opposite, top: Upper High Street, 8 June 1980. After the High Street was pedestrianised in 1976, it created a wide open space as seen here. It is hard to believe, but just a few years earlier this was part of the main thoroughfare from the Ashford–Folkestone/Ashford–Maidstone road. *(Jim Ashby)*

Opposite, bottom: Upper High Street, June 2004. The paving slabs were changed in 1987–8 for brick paviours and new street furniture was installed. *(Steve Salter)*

Upper High Street, 31 August 1980. The shopfront of Marcus Stores is in a sorry state after suffering fire damage, when Matthews' (butchers) signboard (adjacent) caught light. (*Jim Ashby*)

Upper High Street, June 2004. The shopfront of Snappy Snaps at 100 High Street stands proudly in its corporate colours. (*Steve Salter*)

Opposite, top: Lower High Street, October 1971. A superb view of the Lower High Street prior to its redesign. At this time buses used the left-hand side of the High Street while other traffic used the right. It is not until you see a picture of the Lower High Street, pre-pedestrianisation, that you realise how wide the street actually is. (*Jim Ashby*)

Opposite, bottom: Lower High Street, July 2004. A pleasant summer scene showing the traffic-free Lower High Street. The cobbles and York stone were laid in 1999. (*Steve Salter*)

Lower High Street, 19 May 1974. The Lower High Street before traffic was totally banned. *(Jim Ashby)*

Lower High Street, July 2004. Café-culture businesses use outdoor tables and chairs, reminding one of sunny summers abroad in what was once a main road. *(Steve Salter)*

Lower High Street, 19 May 1974. Ashford Odeon, before being converted into a Top Rank and more recently a Mecca bingo hall. Note the old taxis outside. *(Jim Ashby)*

Lower High Street, July 2004. The trees and flowers now create an altogether more pleasant and relaxing setting. *(Steve Salter)*

Lower High Street, 11 April 1976. The bus stops have been moved to what would be the centre of the road to allow for the left-hand side of the Lower High Street to be pedestrianised. *(Jim Ashby)*

Lower High Street, July 2004. Some of the silver birch trees were retained when the High Street was totally pedestrianised in 1999. The parking bays on the right are for disabled parking during the day and for public parking after 6pm. *(Steve Salter)*

High Street/Middle Row, 31 August 1980. Sercombe's gentlemen's and school tailoring and outfitter was for many years at 1a Middle Row. During the 1980s the shop concentrated on menswear and moved to North Street, where the shop closed a few years ago. *(Jim Ashby)*

High Street/Middle Row, July 2004. Ward & Partners, estate agents, now occupy 1a Middle Row. The flowerbeds are still dressed in an attractive manner. *(Steve Salter)*

Lower High Street, 12 September 1976. Prior to its rebuilding the former Headley's Grocer at 46 High Street is seen here soon after its closure. The sign has been painted out, and the sign in the window clearly says that it is for sale or to let. Subsequently the other side of the Headley family, Headley Brothers, the printers, purchased no. 46 and extensively redeveloped the site for their retail stationery business. *(Jim Ashby)*

Lower High Street, July 2004. After the stationery business closed in 1989 after 108 years of the Headley family at no. 46, it was converted into a McDonalds outlet, but with the Headley brothers still the owners. *(Steve Salter)*

Opposite, top: Lower High Street, 28 September 1975. J. Ingall & Son, dispensing chemists, and Photocraft Hi-Fi are seen here at 40 and 42 High Street. *(Jim Ashby)*

Opposite, bottom: Lower High Street, July 2004. Ingalls were later taken over by Paydens Ltd, and in recent years moved to Mill Court opposite Sydenham House surgery. No. 42 is now Private Shop. Photocraft changed its name to Soundcraft in the 1980s when the owners decided to focus on their reputation as audio specialists. *(Steve Salter)*

Lower High Street, 31 August 1980. Halfords were for many years situated at 12 High Street, until 1994 when they moved to a purpose-built superstore at the Warren Retail Park. *(Jim Ashby)*

Lower High Street, July 2004. The former premises of Halfords at no. 12 are now occupied by Sharps Bedrooms. *(Steve Salter)*

Lower High Street, 15 June 1975. The County Hotel stands proud at the bottom of the High Street. Once known as the Fernley Commercial and Temperance Hotel, it was allowed to deteriorate through changing hands perhaps too frequently in the 1980s. It was finally bought by pub chain J.D. Wetherspoon in 1997 and converted into a music-free public house, opening in February 1998. *(Jim Ashby)*

Lower High Street, July 2004. The attractive County Hotel is no longer a hotel but still retains the name. *(Steve Salter)*

Lower High Street, 21 June 1975. Pearl Assurance House shortly after its construction. Previously the site of Olbys, it is situated on the junction of the High Street and Station Road. *(Jim Ashby)*

Lower High Street, July 2004. Pizza Hut is now one of the main occupants of the former Pearl Assurance House, now renamed Northdown House. *(Steve Salter)*

Lower High Street, 1972. A familiar view looking towards Middle Row and St Mary's Church. Babyland & Junior Wear was a popular name for over thirty years. Flinns the cleaners later became the Carvery, a popular lunchtime sandwich bar. *(Lambert Weston)*

Lower High Street, July 2004. The church can barely be seen after the introduction of trees in 1999. A regular street market now operates during weekdays. *(Steve Salter)*

East Hill, 15 June 1975. A rare view of the Star Inn in East Hill under one of its many liveries. To the left the burnt-out shell of East Hill Mill can be seen; the fire there happened a year earlier. *(Jim Ashby)*

East Hill, July 2004. A current view of the Star Inn. East Hill is no longer a thoroughfare. *(Steve Salter)*

New Street, 17 August 1975.
The British Volunteer public
house can be seen here
looking rather dowdy. Next
door, Violet Perkins ran her
general store for many years,
until 1986 when Safeway
supermarket opened opposite.
Her premises were later
demolished for an extension to
Caffyns Garage. *(Jim Ashby)*

New Street, 24 December
1975. Four months later the
public house underwent a
livery change, and also the
addition of an 's' on the end of
Volunteer. Later the 's' was
again dropped. It is not quite
clear why this was done.
(Jim Ashby)

New Street, July 2004.
A summer view of the British
Volunteer under its new
brewery Shepherd Neame.
(Steve Salter)

New Street, 17 August 1975. The Prince of Orange stands prominently at the top of New Street. During the 1980s it was renamed O'Brien's, and became an Irish pub. In 2001 O'Brien's and the derelict Prince Albert next door were extensively refurbished and amalgamated to become the Prince Albert. *(Jim Ashby)*

An attractive view of the Prince Albert, New Street, July 2004. *(Steve Salter)*

Somerset Road, 15 June 1975. The Trumpeter Inn once stood next door to the former Cruden House School alongside the Ringway. It closed in the late 1980s and the premises were derelict for several years afterwards. It was later renovated to become popular pizza takeaway Domino's. *(Jim Ashby)*

Somerset Road, July 2004. Domino's is seen here in a prime position along Somerset Road; they offer a delivery service in the town and surrounding villages. *(Steve Salter)*

Apsley Street, 31 August 1980. The Elephant and Castle was situated at the corner of Apsley Street and Godinton Road. One of Ashford's regular haunts, it was converted to Oranges Bar Café in the early 1990s. The landlord and landlady are those who were the last at the Castle Inn before it closed, Stuart Barton and Dee Martin. *(Jim Ashby)*

Apsley Street, July 2004. Oranges Bar Café is today a busy venue for live music including jazz, folk and popular. *(Steve Salter)*

New Street, 21 June 1975. A sunny day, showing New Street from its junction with Magazine Road. David Easton's TV specialists has for many years occupied the former Greyhound public house, latterly Passmore's the builders' merchants, at 74 New Street. *(Jim Ashby)*

New Street, July 2004. A recent view of New Street, showing the former Caffyn's garage site now redeveloped into three shop units. These are Choices Video, Farm Foods and Topps Tiles. David Easton (left) is still trading today. *(Steve Salter)*

East Hill, 23 April 1989. A blaze destroyed the old provender mill and mill house at East Hill Mill in 1974. When the building was converted into a nightclub a mock waterwheel was made as a feature to replace the one lost in the fire. *(Jim Ashby)*

East Hill, July 2004. Several years ago the mock waterwheel was removed as it had decayed. It was never replaced. Liquid and Life, now a successful nightclub, is owned by Luminar Leisure. *(Steve Salter)*

2

Redevelopment Recollections

Somerset Road, *c.* 1970. A view of the houses demolished for the Ringway and Charter House in 1971. The site was to change drastically shortly after this photograph was taken. *(Lambert Weston)*

Somerset Road, 1971. The roofs of the old properties are seen here being removed shortly before the demolition for the perimeter of the Ringway. *(Jim Ashby)*

Somerset Road, 15 December 1971. The site for the new Ringway and the Charter building has largely been cleared by December of that year. *(Lambert Weston)*

Charter site, 18 October 1972. A view of Charter House in its early stages of construction. *(Lambert Weston)*

Opposite, top: Somerset Road junction with Wellesley Road, 1973. The Charter building has grown and the Ringway is taking shape. You have to feel sorry for the residents of Somerset Road at this time. *(Lambert Weston)*

Opposite, bottom: Somerset Road junction with Wellesley Road, July 2004. Taken from the top of the Crown Building, this view shows the Ringway and Charter House thirty-one years later. *(Steve Salter)*

Somerset Road, 15 December 1971. A dramatic view showing the demolition of these houses ready for redevelopment. It is difficult to imagine what it must have been like to live in the town during this period of reconstruction. *(Lambert Weston)*

Somerset Road, July 2004. The Ringway now forms part of Somerset Road. This view shows its junction with North Street. *(Steve Salter)*

Somerset Road, 22 December 1971. The buildings alongside the Masonic Temple in North Street are seen here being comprehensively demolished. *(Lambert Weston)*

Somerset Road, July 2004. A re-routed Edinburgh Road now passes through as a link to the Ringway. The office building now houses the Kent Messenger Group (Ashford Office), NatWest Business Centre and Lark FM, Ashford's local radio station. *(Steve Salter)*

Somerset Road, 20 December 1971. This dramatic view shows the demolition of houses ready for the construction of the Ringway. *(Lambert Weston)*

Somerset Road, July 2004. The Ringway now passes through where the houses once stood. This is the section from the North Street junction. *(Steve Salter)*

Wellesley Road, 15 December 1971. Hardly recognisable today, this was Wellesley Road at its junction with Somerset Road. Mace Lane now passes from left to right of the picture. Work has yet to begin on Charter House, the site fenced off on the right. *(Lambert Weston)*

Wellesley Road, July 2004. The busy Ringway today, showing the road sweeping from Mace Lane, and the filter lane for Park Street. *(Steve Salter)*

Wellesley Road, *c.* 1970. The houses and businesses in Wellesley Road before their demolition for Charter House and the extension of Park Street. *(Lambert Weston)*

Wellesley Road, July 2004. The Wellesley Road section of the Ringway as it is today. *(Steve Salter)*

Ringway construction, 1974. This rare view shows the Ringway under construction at its junction with North Street. Charter House can be seen nearing completion in the background. *(Jim Ashby)*

Ringway, July 2004. The Ringway today provides a controversial orbital road around the town centre. Plans are being looked at to calm the effects of its racetrack image, and change it for a more favourable design. *(Steve Salter)*

Ringway construction, 1974. The streets that had been severed for the Ringway were still in use until its opening. Park Road can be seen here within the wooden fence. *(Jim Ashby)*

Ringway, July 2004. The flank walls of the properties on the left indicate where whole streets once stood. *(Steve Salter)*

Ringway construction, 1974. This view shows the Ringway at its junction with North Street nearing completion. *(Jim Ashby)*

Ringway, July 2004. Traffic at a halt at the North Street crossing, showing Chambers Garage on the right. *(Steve Salter)*

Above: Wellesley Road, 1973. Houses that had stood for decades are seen here under demolition, to allow the road to be widened. *(Jim Ashby)*

Right: Wellesley Road, 1973. Later in the year, this view shows the site after the houses had been fully cleared. *(Jim Ashby)*

Wellesley Road, 1974. More than a year afterwards the Ringway is starting to take shape. Charter House is almost complete to the right of the photograph. *(Jim Ashby)*

Wellesley Road, July 2004. This view of Wellesley Road from the roof of the Crown Building shows the Ringway as it is today. *(Steve Salter)*

Station Road, July 1971. Looking towards Wellesley Road, the houses and shops to the right of the photograph have already been bulldozed, exposing the Duke of Marlborough public house at the top of East Hill. Many will remember its round turret corner and clock. It was an attractive building, but sadly it too was demolished shortly after this photograph was taken. *(Jim Ashby)*

Station Road, July 2004. The road is much wider than before; this was the reason for demolishing the Duke of Marlborough. Ashford lost many of its public houses during the 1970s. *(Steve Salter)*

North Street, 1972. This row of houses stood next to the Masonic Temple in North Street. The road running alongside is Somerset Road, and on the opposite corner stood the Somerset Arms public house. Shortly afterwards these houses were demolished for the Ringway. *(Lambert Weston)*

North Street, July 2004. The crossing at North Street, where the houses once stood. The building on the right was built in the late 1980s. *(Steve Salter)*

North Street, September 1971. The Lord Roberts public house (previously the Red Lion) is seen sandwiched between 10 and 14 North Street. As part of the road widening scheme, and to create a service road in front of Charter House, sadly the Lord Roberts was demolished two years later. *(Jim Ashby)*

North Street, July 2004. Shoppers pass through the cobbled street where the Lord Roberts once stood. *(Steve Salter)*

Lord Roberts public house, North Street, 1973. The second view showing the yard entrance to the Lord Roberts public house during its dismantling. *(Jim Ashby)*

Park Street, July 2004. This is how the street looks today. *(Steve Salter)*

Opposite, top: Lord Roberts public house, North Street, 1973. One of two views showing the Lord Roberts being dismantled. *(Jim Ashby)*

Opposite, bottom: North Street, July 2004. Looking towards Charter House, the gap is left by the absence of the public house. *(Steve Salter)*

Park Street, 1973. Postman's Row can be seen to the left of the photograph before its demolition for the widening of Park Street. The road to the left was Wolseley Road and the buildings to the right are the rear of Woolworths and Geerings. The Lord Roberts public house can be seen in the distance. *(Jim Ashby)*

Park Street, July 2004. The street now serves the rear of Park Mall Shopping Centre as a service area and there is a taxi rank outside Wilkinsons. *(Steve Salter)*

North Street junction with Park Street, 1972. The premises of John Hogbin & Son, estate agent and auctioneers, are seen to the right alongside J.H. Price, ophthalmic optician. The upper floor of John Hogbins at 5 North Street was once used as offices by Ashford Urban District Council. When the road was widened Hogbins, together with the buildings directly behind it, were demolished. *(Lambert Weston)*

Park Street July, 2004. A view of the widened Park Street looking towards the former Sainsburys, now Wilkinsons. *(Steve Salter)*

North Street, 1972. The Lord Roberts public house and W.H. Gibbs house furnishers are seen here at 12 and 14 North Street. *(Lambert Weston)*

North Street, July 2004. No. 12 has gone, as we have seen, and no. 14 is now the ever-popular Pizza Express. *(Steve Salter)*

Park Street, 1972. A fascinating view of Park Street, showing the rear of Geerings, Woolworths and the International Stores on the left, while Henlys the Wolseley dealer, Postman's Row and R. Dean turf accountant are seen on the right. The street on the right is Edinburgh Road, and further along on the right is Wolseley Road. *(Lambert Weston)*

Park Street, July 2004. Looking totally different today, Park Street was severed by the construction of the Park Mall Shopping Centre in 1986. *(Steve Salter)*

Park Road, *c.* 1970. A forgotten view of Park Road at its junction with Stone Street, looking towards Castle Street. The houses on the left were demolished many years ago, leaving the site open for several years. *(Lambert Weston)*

St George's Square, July 2004. In the foreground the canopy for the tank can be seen. The buildings on the left form part of the Park Mall Shopping Centre. This is approximately where the Park Road houses once stood. *(Steve Salter)*

Charter Site, 25 November 1971. Looking towards the rear of North Street, this is the scene when the site was cleared to start the construction of Charter House. The tall house in the centre is that of Miss Lepard, at 22 North Street. *(Lambert Weston)*

Park Street, July 2004. Park Street service road now passes through the site, together with Charter House on the right. No. 22 North Street can still be seen in the centre. *(Steve Salter)*

Somerset Road junction with Wellesley Road, 1973. This interesting view, from the roof of the Crown Building, shows the Charter site being cleared of trees.
No. 22 North Street can again be seen in the distance. *(Jim Ashby)*

Somerset Road junction with Wellesley Road, July 2004. The imposing structure of Charter House dominates the scene. *(Steve Salter)*

Charter site, 1973. Here the cranes and heavy machinery are seen constructing the foundations of Charter House. *(Jim Ashby)*

Charter House from Wellesley Road, July 2004. Thirty-one years later Stena Line and the Alliance & Leicester occupy most of the Charter building. *(Steve Salter)*

Charter site, 1972. This view was taken by a resident of Somerset Road during construction. A large crater can be seen to the rear of the National Westminster Bank and the Co-op department store. *(Fred Legg)*

Charter House from Somerset Road, July 2004. The residents' view has never been the same since Charter House appeared. Even St Mary's Church is hidden by the building. *(Steve Salter)*

Opposite, top: Charter site, 30 June 1972. An uninterrupted view of Somerset Road before the construction of the Charter building. *(Lambert Weston)*

Opposite, bottom: Charter House, July 2004. Looking across the car park at Charter House towards Somerset Road and the Ringway. *(Steve Salter)*

Charter site, 13 November 1972. Another view of Charter House during the early stages of construction, looking towards Somerset Road. *(Lambert Weston)*

Charter House, July 2004. This image, taken from the same position, shows Charter House as it stands today. *(Steve Salter)*

Charter House, 5 June 1973. A superb view of the Charter building under construction taken from the fire escape, to the rear of the National Westminster Bank. *(Lambert Weston)*

Charter House, July 2004. The giant office complex seen at its best. The car park in the foreground belongs to NatWest Bank. *(Steve Salter)*

Charter House, 1974. Charter House nearing its completion stage, and seen from the roof of the Crown building. *(Jim Ashby)*

Charter House, July 2004. This is the view from the corner of Wellesley Road and Mace Lane. *(Steve Salter)*

Godinton Road, 20 December 1971. Before the Ringway was made one-way, this section in Godinton Road was two-way for a short period. The Elephant and Castle public house can be seen on the right, on the corner of Apsley Street. *(Lambert Weston)*

Godinton Road/Ringway, July 2004. Here we are looking towards West Street and Forge Lane. *(Steve Salter)*

Godinton Road junction with Apsley Street, 1971. Another view showing the construction of this section of the Ringway. The Elephant and Castle public house is on the right and Gasworks Lane on the left. *(Lambert Weston)*

Godinton Road junction with Apsley Street, July 2004. The houses on the right were demolished in the early 1970s and the Elephant and Castle public house is now Oranges Bar Café. *(Steve Salter)*

West Street/Forge Lane, 10 April 1974. Seen from Godinton Road, this view shows the Ringway under construction looking towards the Telephone Exchange in Regents Place. *(Lambert Weston)*

West Street/Forge Lane, July 2004. The same section of the Ringway as it looks today. *(Steve Salter)*

New Street, March 1973. An early view after the houses were demolished in New Street to allow the road widening for the Ringway scheme. *(Lambert Weston)*

New Street junction with the Ringway, July 2004. The scene today, looking towards Lidl supermarket and Norwood Gardens. *(Steve Salter)*

3

Gridlock before the Ringway

Bank Street, 7 July 1964. This nostalgic view was taken for a survey, prior to the building of the Ringway. It shows how busy the town centre could be during weekdays. *(Ashford Borough Council)*

Bank Street, July 2004. Forty years later, still used by traffic, the street is not as busy as it once was. This is partly because of the surrounding Ringway. *(Steve Salter)*

Bank Street, 7 July 1964. The Market Hotel can be clearly seen on the left-hand side on the corner of Godinton Road. The bus is heading for Boughton Lees and Kennington – a double-decker is a rare sight in the town nowadays. The building on the right was then the Corn Exchange. (*Ashford Borough Council*)

Bank Street, July 2004. The Market Hotel, later the Wig and Gavel, was demolished in the early 1990s. The site is earmarked for redevelopment later in 2004, to create an extension to County Square Shopping Centre. (*Steve Salter*)

Bank Street, 7 July 1964. Busy with traffic, this picture was taken around midday and shows a double-decker bus negotiating its way into the High Street, at the top of the picture. *(Ashford Borough Council)*

Bank Street July, 2004. The top of Bank Street is now pedestrianised, providing access only for disabled drivers and delivery vehicles. The pedestrianised area is open to through traffic in the evenings, however. *(Steve Salter)*

Bank Street junction with High Street, July 1964. This is one of two views from the upper floor of Burtons tailors. It shows the traffic jams of the 1960s. Given the increasing volumes of traffic since then, it would be extremely troublesome if the High Street was still a through road in 2004. *(Ashford Borough Council)*

Bank Street junction with High Street, 7 July 1964. Another image of the gridlock in the town centre at that time. *(Ashford Borough Council)*

Bank Street junction with High Street, 2004. This is the High Street today, with the performance area to the right. *(Steve Salter)*

Main image: High Street junction with Bank Street, 9 July 1964. These are the queues of traffic entering the town centre at 9.50a.m. *(Ashford Borough Council)*

Inset: High Street junction with Bank Street, July 2004. Traffic can still be seen. Disabled drivers are permitted, but the street is far quieter than before. *(Steve Salter)*

Upper High Street, 7 July 1964. In this view from an upper floor window in King's Parade, traffic is seen entering the town from the A20. Incidentally the white single-decker bus belongs to Maidstone & District Bus Co. *(Ashford Borough Council)*

Upper High Street, July 2004. This is the performance area and street market. The introduction of tree planting has made an attractive alternative to the queuing traffic. *(Steve Salter)*

Upper High Street, 10 July 1964. This superb view of the Upper High Street where it meets Castle Street shows the queuing traffic at 8.56 on a Friday morning. *(Ashford Borough Council)*

Upper High Street, July 2004. Today's peaceful setting of the Upper High Street. It is difficult to imagine what it would be like with traffic flowing through today. *(Steve Salter)*

Castle Street, 10 July 1964. This view shows the difficulty lorries and vans had negotiating their way past the Castle Hotel in 1964. Even today the Castle (now the Halifax) regularly has its shopfront damaged by delivery vehicles. *(Ashford Borough Council)*

Castle Street, July 2004. Again no traffic, which makes life much easier for shoppers. *(Steve Salter)*

High Street, 9 July 1964. Delivery lorries stop outside Marks & Spencers, Boots the Chemist and Vye & Son, the grocer. The Saracen's Head Hotel (demolished in 1966) is on the right. *(Ashford Borough Council)*

High Street, July 2004. The pedestrianised area forty years later. *(Steve Salter)*

High Street junction with North Street, July 1964. This is a typical 1960s street scene in Ashford. *(Ashford Borough Council)*

High Street junction with North Street, July 2004. An ambulance negotiates its way through the pedestrianised area. Boots the Chemist (previously Sainsburys) is on the right. *(Steve Salter)*

North Street, July 1964. Double-decker buses pass each other outside Ashley Russell and the Saracen's Head Hotel. *(Ashford Borough Council)*

North Street, July 2004. North Street is now one-way in the direction of Kennington, and contains buildings in a conservation area. The building on the right, Boots, occupies less space than its predecessor. The Saracen's Head Hotel left little space for traffic especially double-decker buses, with its close proximity to the road. *(Steve Salter)*

North Street, July 2004. Nowadays North Street has a mixture of restaurants, offices and specialist shops. This view looks towards Kennington. *(Steve Salter)*

Opposite, top: North Street, 9 July 1964. A double-decker bus approaches the traffic lights in North Street. The building on the right was for many years the Fifty-Shilling Tailor. Dennes the Seed Merchants can be seen along on the right. *(Ashford Borough Council)*

Opposite, bottom: North Street, 9 July 1964. This tanker is turning left into the High Street from North Street. *(Ashford Borough Council)*

Lower High Street, 1964. The wide High Street can be seen clearly from this position at the top of East Hill. Buses pull up outside the County Hotel, and traffic can be seen heading towards the centre of town on the left-hand side. *(Ashford Borough Council)*

Lower High Street, 2004. *(Steve Salter)*

Station Road, 9 July 1964. A rare view of Station Road. The Baptist church can be seen on the left, behind the road sign. At the top of the picture a bus can be seen coming from the junction of the High Street and East Hill. The shops and houses on the right were later demolished for the Ringway. *(Ashford Borough Council)*

Station Road, July 2004. A busy Ringway scene, looking towards Wellesley Road and the High Street. The brightened-up Baptist church can again be seen on the left. *(Steve Salter)*

Opposite: East Hill, 2 July 1964. Before the arrival of the Ringway East Hill and Hythe Road formed the main road from Ashford to Folkestone. Traffic can be seen here passing the Duke of Marlborough public house and the Ashford School buildings. *(Ashford Borough Council)*

Right: East Hill, 2 July 1964. A view further to the right, showing Hoskins the Tobacconist advertising Woodbine cigarettes. The Duke of Marlborough and Hoskins were later demolished for the Ringway. *(Ashford Borough Council)*

Below: East Hill, July 2004. East Hill is now dominated by Ashford School. It is no longer a through road. *(Steve Salter)*

East Hill, 9 July 1964. A view looking towards the High Street with Ashford School premises on both sides of the road. *(Ashford Borough Council)*

East Hill, July 2004. It was deserted, apart from one lady who seemed to enjoy being photographed. *(Steve Salter)*

Elwick Road, 3 July 1964. An excellent view looking towards Bank Street. The former Royal Mail sorting office can be seen on the right and the old South Kent College buildings are next door. The cyclist seems to have the right idea. *(Ashford Borough Council)*

Elwick Road, July 2004. The one-way traffic flow of Ashford Ringway, looking towards Bank Street. The black-and-white timber building has recently been vacated by Kent Social Services, who have moved into the Civic Centre at Tannery Lane. *(Steve Salter)*

Elwick Road, 9 July 1964. Looking towards Station Road, this picture shows queuing traffic at 5.40p.m. The Kent Arms public house can be seen in the distance. *(Ashford Borough Council)*

Elwick Road, July 2004. Again, the traffic flow has been reversed in Elwick Road. Kudos nightclub can be seen alongside Ashford railway station in the distance. *(Steve Salter)*

4

All Change on the Landmark Front

East Hill Mill, September 1971. This is East Hill (Pledge's) Mill three years before a major fire destroyed the older mill buildings. The white-boarded provender mill, and the miller's house to the right, was destroyed in the blaze in May 1974. Sadly the burnt-out shell of the older buildings was demolished, as they were deemed unsafe. The six-storey tower still survives today. *(Jim Ashby)*

East Hill Mill, July 2004. The smaller mill was rebuilt in 1981 and became Ashford's first nightclub Dusty's, and then the Jolly Miller. It has been a nightclub ever since then and is now known as Liquid and Life. *(Steve Salter)*

East Hill Mill, 16 May 1974. This highly dramatic view illustrates the last moments of the old provender mill. *(Jim Ashby)*

East Hill Mill, July 2004. The replacement extension, which was built in 1981. *(Steve Salter)*

East Hill Mill, 19 May 1974. The aftermath of the blaze, showing the full extent of the damage to the six-storey tower and the remains of the provender mill. The remains in the foreground were demolished shortly after this time. (Jim Ashby)

East Hill Mill, July 2004. The renovated mill as it looks today. (Steve Salter)

Opposite, top: East Hill Mill, 16 May 1974. The main provender mill is seen shortly after its collapse. Firemen are still battling to get the blaze under control. (Jim Ashby)

Opposite, bottom: East Hill, July 2004. This is the scene today, showing the forecourt to the nightclub. (Steve Salter)

Hempsted Street, 15 June 1975. The Invicta public house was one of Ashford's many popular pubs, situated at the Godinton Road end of Hempsted Street. *(Jim Ashby)*

Hempsted Street, July 2004. The Invicta was demolished in the early 1990s to make way for a car park. The site is to be redeveloped as part of an extension to County Square Shopping Centre. *(Steve Salter)*

Bank Street, 15 June 1975. The Market Hotel stood at the corner of Bank Street and Godinton Road. It was later renamed the Wig & Gavel. The remaining section of wall which once formed the frontage of Stanhay's can be seen on the left. *(Jim Ashby)*

The pub on 13 July 1980. The site was earmarked for redevelopment and the building was demolished in the early 1990s. *(Jim Ashby)*

Bank Street, July 2004. The car park where the Wig & Gavel once stood. *(Steve Salter)*

Beaver Road, 11 January 1976. The Victoria Hotel stood for many years on the corner of Beaver Road and Victoria Road. Next door was the Butchers Hotel, which suffered a fire in the mid-1980s. The Victoria was run by licensees Stuart Barton and Dee Martin until it was lined up for demolition, in the late 1990s. *(Jim Ashby)*

Beaver Road, July 2004. The site is now cordoned off by a screen, awaiting redevelopment. *(Steve Salter)*

Beaver Road, 14 March 1976. The Cinema once stood on the corner of Newtown Road and Beaver Road. Once known as the Royal, it stood opposite the Butchers Hotel. To the right John Wiliment, the Ford dealership, operated for many years, in what was later to become a B&Q Supercentre. *(Jim Ashby)*

Beaver Road, 31 January 1988. Another view of the cinema, when it had acquired the title of the Picture House. Next door to the right were Kwik-Fit Euro and the B&Q Supercentre. The cinema shut its doors for the last time in 1992 and was later demolished to make way for a roundabout. *(Jim Ashby)*

Beaver Road, July 2004. This is the roundabout that replaced the cinema. *(Steve Salter)*

Beaver Road, 1974. A closer view of The Cinema in 1974. *(Lambert Weston)*

Beaver Road, July 2004. This is part of the orbital road that has replaced Newtown Road, which ran alongside the former cinema. *(Steve Salter)*

Opposite, top: Maidstone Road, 11 April 1977. The Roman Catholic Church of St Teresa of Avila was designed by Edward Pugin, and stood on the site for many years. It was demolished in the 1980s and replaced with the building below. *(Jim Ashby)*

Opposite, bottom: Maidstone Road, July 2004. The replacement St Teresa's is seen behind the trees. The church is dramatically different from its predecessor, with its very modern design. *(Steve Salter)*

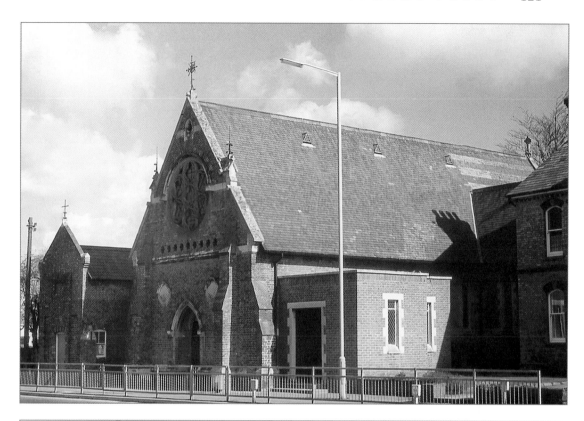

Ashford station, 25 March 1974. This is the former Ashford station and car park before redevelopment in the 1990s, to create an international station for Ashford. *(Lambert Weston)*

Ashford station, July 2004. The present domestic and international station complex showing the new buildings and the High Speed Rail Link. Ashford is the only official Eurostar station in the UK, apart from Waterloo. *(Steve Salter)*

5

Remember When . . .

St George's Square, 6 July 1973. This splendid photograph has New Street, the main road from Ashford to Maidstone, disappearing into the distance, and the First World War tank, which was given to the town on 1 August 1919, on the right. *(Lambert Weston)*

St George's Square, July 2004. Now pedestrianised, the street is still busy with delivery vehicles and shoppers. *(Steve Salter)*

St George's Square, 4 May 1972. The tank is seen outside the Old Prince of Wales public house, and the New China City Restaurant. For many years the tank housed an electricity sub-station. *(Jim Ashby)*

St George's Square, July 2004. The tank as it is today, protected by a canopy which was built in 1988. *(Steve Salter)*

Park Road, *c.* 1970. Park Road ran from Castle Street to Albert Road until the Ringway divided it. On the left are the New China City Restaurant, the 3 Day Cleaners and the Vacuum Centre, and on the right is the Folkestone Glass Works. *(Lambert Weston)*

St George's Square, July 2004. All the buildings on the right are now part of Park Mall Shopping Centre; the houses and businesses were demolished several years ago. *(Steve Salter)*

Castle Street, 1974. Castle Street, looking towards the High Street, when buildings, including Charles Warner the butcher, Frank Palmer the gents' outfitter and Kingsman's the baker, were being demolished for the Tufton Shopping Centre. *(Jim Ashby)*

Castle Street, July 2004. Marks & Spencer's new store was built in place of the building in the photograph above. Apart from the changing businesses Castle Street looks much the same today. *(Steve Salter)*

St George's Square, 1957.
The predecessor to Folkestone Glass
Works was Ashford Cleaners Ltd
in their rather battered building on
the corner of Park Road and Park
Street. *(Lambert Weston)*

Park Road, 1970. Folkestone
Glass Works are seen here in
the improved and enlarged
building several years later.
It was further extended to
create a showroom in 1974.
(Lambert Weston)

St George's Square, July 2004.
The attractive buildings of Park
Mall Shopping Centre have
replaced the previous buildings.
(Steve Salter)

Kings Parade, 28 March 1974. This is a familiar view to many. Parking was then allowed in the High Street and shops including Dixons ironmongers and Bodshams greengrocers were still trading. *(Lambert Weston)*

Kings Parade, July 2004. Flowerbeds and a street market replace the once traffic-dominated street. *(Steve Salter)*

Upper High Street, 1972, after Lewis & Hyland's and W.H. Gibbs's premises had been demolished. *(Lambert Weston)*

Upper High Street, July 2004. This is now the scene of a bustling market. *(Steve Salter)*

Bank Street, May 1953. A splendid view of the offices of Hallett & Co. Solicitors and the Royal Insurance Company Limited, which later moved to the corner of Bank Street and Tufton Street. The shop to the right of the photograph was G. Herbert the jeweller. It later became the Turntable record store and latterly Richards Records. They only occupied half of the original jewellers; the other half was for many years the premises of Country Ways health foods. *(Weavers/Countrywide)*

Bank Street, June 2004. The row of delightful buildings remains much the same today. The former Royal Insurance Offices were later remodelled in the style of the existing building to form part of the solicitors' offices. *(Steve Salter)*

St George's Square, 1957. An unusual view of St George's Square, looking towards Park Road. Taken from the upper floor of Goddard's the butchers, it shows the tank before its protective cover was built. The Old Prince of Wales public house can be seen on the left. At this time it was owned by the reputable Kentish brewer Fremlins, later to become part of the Whitbread Group. The road running from left to right in the foreground is New Street. In 1957 this was still the main road from the coast to London. *(Lambert Weston)*

St George's Square, June 2004. Much has changed over the years. Park Road was obliterated by the construction of the Park Mall Shopping Centre in 1987, although the houses were demolished in the late 1970s. The square has also since been pedestrianised, creating a pleasant seating area for both the public house and visitors to the town. *(Steve Salter)*

North Street, 1973. A busy street scene at a time when North Street was still a main thoroughfare. No. 22 North Street can be seen on the left with a lady leaving by the front door. The Lepard sisters occupied this property for many years, and a large section of their rear garden was sold to Charter Consolidated for their office construction. The Lord Roberts public house can be seen to the right, next to Dennes the Seed Merchants, (the building with the tall chimney). Shortly after the photograph was taken the Lord Roberts was demolished for the realignment of Park Street. *(Lambert Weston)*

North Street, June 2004. North Street is now much quieter than it was thirty-one years ago. It could be classed as a 'restaurant dominated' street, having Turkish, Indian, Italian and Chinese eating places among its buildings. *(Steve Salter)*

North Street, 1973. A dramatic view taken through a broken window, from a soon-to-be-demolished property in North Street. Again it is clear that traffic was once a familiar sight and that since pedestrianisation North Street has become very much quieter. The Leyland National single-decker buses were for many years an everyday sight in the town, negotiating their way around Ashford's narrow streets. They disappeared in the late 1980s when they were replaced by smaller more manageable buses. The North Street car park can be seen on the right. It was later sold for redevelopment. *(Lambert Weston)*

North Street, June 2004.
The attractive traffic-free
thoroughfare is seen from the
upper floor offices, which now
occupy the former car park site.
(Steve Salter)

North Street, 1970. Another view of a 'traffic strewn' North Street. The building on the right was at the time occupied by Harrison Clague, architect, and Dresden ladies' hairdresser. Further along, the white-faced building was for many years Fendall's the wine merchant. During its restoration by Charter Consolidated in the following years, it was found that the top floor windows were false. They were later put to use when an extra floor was built. The church of St Mary's can be seen in the distance. *(Lambert Weston)*

North Street, June 2004. Little has changed with regard to the buildings in North Street, all of which were renovated by Charter Consolidated in the early 1970s. *(Steve Salter)*

North Street, 1970. A splendid view of the premises of Harrison Clague the architect and Dresden hairdressers. The building is timber framed and is mainly hung with mathematical tiles. It was once a subject of interest to local historian Walter Briscall, who described the building in great architectural detail in his *Discovering Ashford's Old Buildings. (Lambert Weston)*

North Street, June 2004. This is now one of Ashford's conservation areas. *(Steve Salter)*

North Street, 1962. An S class Jaguar sits proudly outside 22 North Street, possibly a visitor for the Lepard sisters. *(Lambert Weston)*

North Street, June 2004. No. 22 has now been converted into individual flats: a far cry from a once grand town house but the exterior still looks splendid. *(Steve Salter)*

North Street, 1970. Although still a main thoroughfare, there is no sign of traffic. John Hogbin, estate agents, can be seen to the immediate left. Next door is J.H. Price, ophthalmic optician, which later became Cargills but still retained J.H. Price as the optician. The building opposite was for many years occupied by W.H. Gibbs, the house furnishers and removal contractors. They formerly had a shop in the High Street and a separate carpet shop a few doors away. They moved to North Street when their High Street premises had to make way for the Tufton Shopping Centre. Further along on the right is the Olde Cottage Restaurant, whose original signage was painted by the late Walter Briscall. *(Lambert Weston)*

North Street, June 2004. Pizza Express now occupies the former Gibbs showroom. John Hogbin, estate agent, was demolished in 1973 to allow the widening of Park Street. *(Steve Salter)*

North Street, 1970. *(Lambert Weston)*

North Street, June 2004. The flank wall of Top Notch still shows the roofline of the Lord Roberts pub. *(Steve Salter)*

Left: Somerset Road, 1961. In the distance the junction with Wellesley Road can be seen. These houses together with those in Wellesley Road were demolished ten years later when work began on the Ringway. (*Lambert Weston*)

Right: Somerset Road, June 2004. Concrete and tarmac now replace the elegant houses which were once part of Somerset Road. Charter House can be seen on the right. (*Steve Salter*)

Left: Somerset Road junction with North Street, 1973. At this time Somerset Road was one-way in the opposite direction to that of today. The Somerset Arms public house can be seen on the right opposite a not-instantly-recognisable Chambers Garage. The thoroughfare alongside Chambers is Blue Line Lane, which ran from Magazine Road, to North Street. On construction of the Ringway, the scene illustrated here disappeared. (*Lambert Weston*)

Right: Somerset Road, June 2004. The garage still remains, and the black-and-white timber building can still be picked out thirty-one years later. All else has changed and one doesn't take the time to remember what stood there before the Ringway. (*Steve Salter*)

Elwick Road, 1971. An early view of the Elwick Road section of the Ringway, shortly after its opening. Ashford Market can be seen on the left. To the right Stanhay's car showroom once dominated Elwick Road and its junction with Bank Street. The building in the centre was once the home of the Brown family, owners of Gerald Brown the greengrocer in New Rents. *(Lambert Weston)*

Elwick Road, June 2004. The Stanhay buildings are long gone, and Ashford Market moved out of town several years ago. This section of Elwick Road is now the subject of plans for traffic calming once the extension to County Square Shopping Centre is completed. *(Steve Salter)*

Mace Lane, 1974. These three views of Mace Lane tell their own little story. On research and closer inspection one finds that the first view was taken on 17 May 1974, the day after the fire at the flour mill in the distance. As we have seen, the mill suffered extensive damage; the older provender mill collapsed into the road. East Hill served as part of the main Folkestone to Ashford road at the time, and Folkestone-bound traffic used Mace Lane. The incomplete carriageway of Mace Lane can be clearly seen and could not be used to divert traffic from East Hill. So one side of Mace Lane was made two-way, while the rubble was cleared from the flour mill. In the other two photographs, the smouldering mill has disappeared and other carriageway of Mace Lane has been finished. An eventful few days for Ashfordians! *(Jim Ashby/Lambert Weston)*

Opposite, top and centre: Ashford Market, 1972. These two splendid views show the once thriving market before its departure from the town. The fashions of 1972 are obvious in these pictures. It was a sad day for many when the market finally closed, eventually to give way to Kvaerner and their contractors, who have since used the former market site as their base for the Channel Tunnel Rail Link offices. *(Jim Ashby)*

Opposite, bottom: Former Ashford Market site, June 2004. The site is now subject to high security, to deter saboteurs during the continuing construction. *(Steve Salter)*

ACKNOWLEDGEMENTS

Over the years many local people and companies have been extremely kind and patient in assisting me with my research. Many have given me very valuable information which has enabled me to collate an interesting record of the history of Ashford and build a substantial photographic collection. Since the publication of my first book *Changing Ashford* last year, I have received much kindness from people who have allowed me to use their pictures. I would therefore like to give special thanks to the following individuals and companies:

Richard Filmer of Halifax Property Services, Jim Ashby photographer; Cllr Allen Wells, Mayor of Ashford; Arthur Coleman, Mike Bennett, Dave Downey and Barry Hollis at the Kent Messenger Group; Ben Grabham, Lois Jarrett, Adrian Westwood and Ray Wilkinson at Ashford Borough Council; Kent Regional Newspapers (Ashford office); Ottakars; W.H. Smith; Sussex Stationers, Ashford; David 'Taffy' James at Berkeley Estates (Charter House); Betty Shadwell, Dennis Fricker and Alan Terry at Ashford Borough Museum; Tracey McKeen and staff at Ashford TIC; Brenda and George Sharp; the late Tom Hall and his wife Mollie; Richard Carley, photographer; Clague Architects; the late Walter Briscall; Roland and Alan Yeung; Tony and team of T&D Building and Plastering Specialists (Sittingbourne); James Adams, Shirley Sheridan, Linda Robards and Fiona Hukins at Ashford Library; Phil Neumann at Foto Flite, Ian Gambrill of Countrywide Photographic (Charing Hill); the late Colin Harding of Campbell Reith and Hill; the late Dennis Shadwell, celebrated photographer with the Kent Messenger Group; Richard Stafford and all at Colyer Commercial; Lyn Sumner, Chris West and Sue Gatward at Ashford Town Centre Partnership; former Cllr Gordon Turner; Don Entwistle at CIN Properties; Roy and Maureen Entwistle; Donald and Margaret Samuel; Adrian Brown, Will Kenny and Rob Prince at Luminar Leisure (Liquid and Life, Ashford); Jonathan D. Barrett; Sue Barrett-Austen; Richard Austen; Chris Barrett; Adam Reed; Jerry Ford; Diane and Paul Gooderidge; Andy Summers; Jenny Summers; Tony Matthews; Dave Fox.

Thanks are also due to anyone whose name has not been acknowledged either through an oversight or because the original source or present ownership is unknown or unavailable. I must also thank Kevin and Neil at Snappy Snaps Photo Specialists in Ashford, for their endless help and first-class quality printing. They are always very patient and are true professionals. And finally a big thank you once again to Simon Fletcher and his team at Sutton Publishing for making this second book happen and for being extremely kind throughout.